# Dinosaurs

# Spinosaurus

by Julie Murray

1

## Dash!
### LEVELED READERS
An Imprint of Abdo Zoom • abdobooks.com

# Dash!
## LEVELED READERS

**Level 1 – Beginning**
Short and simple sentences with familiar words or patterns for children who are beginning to understand how letters and sounds go together.

**Level 2 – Emerging**
Longer words and sentences with more complex language patterns for readers who are practicing common words and letter sounds.

**Level 3 – Transitional**
More developed language and vocabulary for readers who are becoming more independent.

THIS BOOK CONTAINS RECYCLED MATERIALS

## abdobooks.com

Published by Abdo Zoom, a division of ABDO, PO Box 398166, Minneapolis, Minnesota 55439.
Copyright © 2023 by Abdo Consulting Group, Inc. International copyrights reserved in all countries.
No part of this book may be reproduced in any form without written permission from the publisher.
Dash!™ is a trademark and logo of Abdo Zoom.

Printed in the United States of America, North Mankato, Minnesota.
052022
092022

Photo Credits: Getty Images, Science Source, Shutterstock
Production Contributors: Kenny Abdo, Jennie Forsberg, Grace Hansen, John Hansen
Design Contributors: Candice Keimig, Neil Klinepier

## Library of Congress Control Number: 2021950307

## Publisher's Cataloging in Publication Data

Names: Murray, Julie, author.
Title: Spinosaurus / by Julie Murray
Description: Minneapolis, Minnesota : Abdo Zoom, 2023 | Series: Dinosaurs | Includes online resources and index.
Identifiers: ISBN 9781098228293 (lib. bdg.) | ISBN 9781098229139 (ebook) | ISBN 9781098229559 (Read-to-Me ebook)
Subjects: LCSH: Spinosaurus--Juvenile literature. | Dinosaurs--Juvenile literature. | Paleontology--Juvenile literature. | Extinct animals--Juvenile literature.
Classification: DDC 567.90--dc23

# Table of Contents

# Spinosaurus

Spinosaurus was a **theropod**. It lived 95 million years ago.

It was the largest meat-eating dinosaur to ever live. It was longer and heavier than Tyrannosaurus rex!

Spinosaurus was 60 feet (18.2 m) long. It weighed up to 35,000 pounds (15,875 kg)!

It had a big skull. Its **snout** was long. It looked like a crocodile's mouth.

Spinosaurus mainly walked on two back legs. Its arms were short. It had a long tail.

The dinosaur had tall spines on its back. The spines were connected by skin. This formed a sail.

Spinosaurus lived on land, but was a good swimmer. It hunted on land and in the water.

Spinosaurus ate other dinosaurs and large fish.

Its **fossils** were first
discovered in Egypt in 1912.
German **paleontologist** Ernst
Stromer and his team found
the remains.

# More Facts

- *Spinosaurus* means "spined lizard."

- It could run up to 15 mph (24.1 kph). That is fast for a big dinosaur!

- Its spines were up to seven feet (2.1 m) tall.

22

# Glossary

**fossil** – the remains or trace of a living animal or plant from a long time ago. Fossils are found embedded in earth or rock.

**paleontologist** – a scientist who studies animal and plant fossils for information about life in the past.

**snout** – the front part of an animal's head that sticks out. The snout includes the nose, mouth, and jaws.

**theropod** – a meat-eating dinosaur of a group whose members are typically two-legged and range from small and delicately built to very large.

# Index

# Online Resources

**Booklinks**
**NONFICTION NETWORK**
FREE! ONLINE NONFICTION RESOURCES

To learn more about Spinosaurus, please visit **abdobooklinks.com** or scan this QR code. These links are routinely monitored and updated to provide the most current information available.